CH00842337

MY LITTLE IDEABOOK

Creativity is intelligence having fun.

PAGE	IDEA
1	
2	
3	
4	
5	
6	
7	
8	
9	
10	
11	
12	
13	
14	
15	
16	
17	
18	
19	
20	

21

22

23

24

25

26

27

28

29

30

31

32

33

34

35

36

37

38

39

40

41

42

43

44

45

46

47

48

49

50

51

52

53

54

55

56

57

58

59

60

61

62

63

64

65

66

67

68

69

70

71

72

73

74

75

76

77

78

79

80

81

82

83

84

85

86

87

88

89

90

91

92

93

94

95

96

97

98

99

100

STORY   INVENTION   INNOVATION

☐   ☐   ☐

DATE

_____

2

STORY ☐   INVENTION ☐   INNOVATION ☐

DATE

_____

4

STORY ☐ INVENTION ☐ INNOVATION ☐

DATE

_____

STORY INVENTION INNOVATION
☐ ☐ ☐

DATE

_____

6

STORY ☐ INVENTION ☐ INNOVATION ☐

DATE

_____

STORY   INVENTION   INNOVATION
☐   ☐   ☐

DATE

_____

STORY   INVENTION   INNOVATION

☐   ☐   ☐

DATE

_____

STORY ☐ INVENTION ☐ INNOVATION ☐

DATE
_____

10

STORY ☐ INVENTION ☐ INNOVATION ☐

DATE

_____

11

STORY   INVENTION   INNOVATION
☐   ☐   ☐

DATE

_____

STORY ☐ INVENTION ☐ INNOVATION ☐

DATE
_____

13

STORY ☐   INVENTION ☐   INNOVATION ☐

DATE

_____

14

STORY ☐ INVENTION ☐ INNOVATION ☐

DATE

_____

STORY INVENTION INNOVATION
☐   ☐   ☐

DATE

_____

16

STORY ☐ INVENTION ☐ INNOVATION ☐

DATE

_____

STORY   INVENTION   INNOVATION
☐   ☐   ☐

DATE

_____

18

STORY ☐ INVENTION ☐ INNOVATION ☐

DATE

_____

19

STORY INVENTION INNOVATION
□ □ □

DATE

_____

20

STORY ☐ INVENTION ☐ INNOVATION ☐

DATE

_____

21

STORY   INVENTION   INNOVATION

☐   ☐   ☐

DATE

_____

STORY ☐   INVENTION ☐   INNOVATION ☐

DATE

_____

23

STORY   INVENTION   INNOVATION

☐   ☐   ☐

DATE

_____

25

STORY   INVENTION   INNOVATION
☐   ☐   ☐

DATE

_____

26

STORY ☐   INVENTION ☐   INNOVATION ☐

DATE

_____

27

STORY ☐   INVENTION ☐   INNOVATION ☐

DATE

_____

28

STORY   INVENTION   INNOVATION
☐   ☐   ☐

DATE

_____

STORY □   INVENTION □   INNOVATION □

DATE

_____

30

STORY ☐ INVENTION ☐ INNOVATION ☐

DATE

_____

31

STORY ☐   INVENTION ☐   INNOVATION ☐

DATE

_____

STORY ☐ INVENTION ☐ INNOVATION ☐

DATE

_____

33

STORY ☐   INVENTION ☐   INNOVATION ☐

DATE

_____

34

STORY　　INVENTION　INNOVATION
☐　　　　☐　　　　☐

DATE

_____

STORY   INVENTION   INNOVATION

☐   ☐   ☐

DATE

_____

STORY ☐ INVENTION ☐ INNOVATION ☐

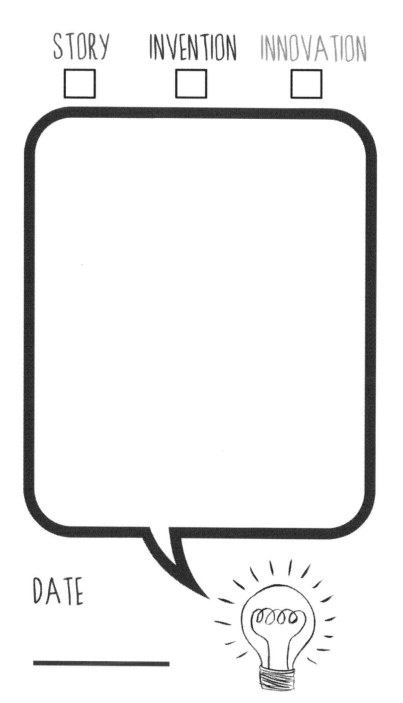

DATE

_____

STORY ☐   INVENTION ☐   INNOVATION ☐

DATE

_____

38

STORY ☐   INVENTION ☐   INNOVATION ☐

DATE

_____

39

STORY ☐   INVENTION ☐   INNOVATION ☐

DATE

_____

40

STORY ☐ INVENTION ☐ INNOVATION ☐

DATE

41

STORY ☐ INVENTION ☐ INNOVATION ☐

DATE

42

STORY ☐   INVENTION ☐   INNOVATION ☐

DATE

43

STORY ☐   INVENTION ☐   INNOVATION ☐

DATE

_____

44

STORY ☐   INVENTION ☐   INNOVATION ☐

DATE

_____

45

STORY   INVENTION   INNOVATION
☐   ☐   ☐

DATE

_____

STORY ☐   INVENTION ☐   INNOVATION ☐

DATE

_____

STORY ☐ INVENTION ☐ INNOVATION ☐

DATE

_____

48

STORY ☐ INVENTION ☐ INNOVATION ☐

DATE

_____

49

STORY ☐   INVENTION ☐   INNOVATION ☐

DATE

_____

50

STORY □   INVENTION □   INNOVATION □

DATE

_____

STORY   INVENTION   INNOVATION
☐   ☐   ☐

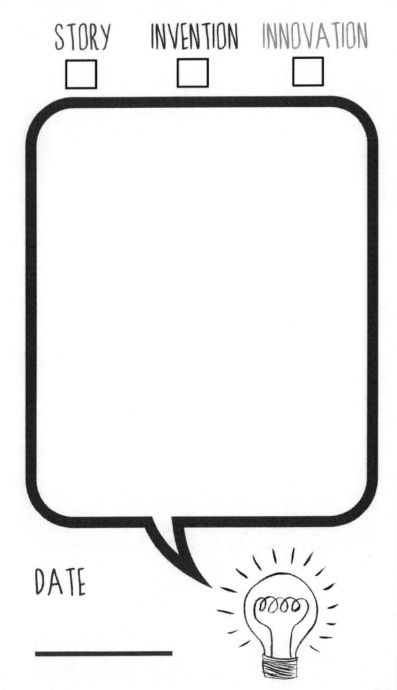

DATE

_____

52

STORY ☐ INVENTION ☐ INNOVATION ☐

DATE

_____

53

STORY ☐   INVENTION ☐   INNOVATION ☐

DATE

54

STORY   INVENTION   INNOVATION
☐   ☐   ☐

DATE

_____

STORY   INVENTION   INNOVATION
☐   ☐   ☐

DATE

_____

STORY ☐ INVENTION ☐ INNOVATION ☐

DATE

_____

57

STORY ☐ INVENTION ☐ INNOVATION ☐

DATE

_____

58

STORY ☐   INVENTION ☐   INNOVATION ☐

DATE

_____

59

STORY ☐   INVENTION ☐   INNOVATION ☐

DATE

_____

STORY ☐ INVENTION ☐ INNOVATION ☐

DATE

_____

STORY ☐   INVENTION ☐   INNOVATION ☐

DATE

_____

62

STORY ☐ INVENTION ☐ INNOVATION ☐

DATE

_____

63

STORY ☐   INVENTION ☐   INNOVATION ☐

DATE

_____

STORY ☐ INVENTION ☐ INNOVATION ☐

DATE

_____

65

STORY   INVENTION   INNOVATION
☐   ☐   ☐

DATE

_____

STORY ☐ INVENTION ☐ INNOVATION ☐

DATE

_____

67

STORY ☐ INVENTION ☐ INNOVATION ☐

DATE

_____

STORY ☐   INVENTION ☐   INNOVATION ☐

DATE

_____

69

STORY   INVENTION   INNOVATION
☐   ☐   ☐

DATE

_____

STORY ☐   INVENTION ☐   INNOVATION ☐

DATE

_____

STORY INVENTION INNOVATION

☐ ☐ ☐

DATE

_____

72

STORY ☐ INVENTION ☐ INNOVATION ☐

DATE

_____

73

STORY ☐   INVENTION ☐   INNOVATION ☐

DATE _____

74

STORY ☐ INVENTION ☐ INNOVATION ☐

DATE

_____

75

STORY ☐   INVENTION ☐   INNOVATION ☐

DATE

_____

76

STORY ☐ INVENTION ☐ INNOVATION ☐

DATE

_____

STORY   INVENTION   INNOVATION
☐   ☐   ☐

DATE

_____

78

STORY ☐ INVENTION ☐ INNOVATION ☐

DATE

79

STORY ☐ INVENTION ☐ INNOVATION ☐

DATE
_____

80

STORY INVENTION INNOVATION

☐ ☐ ☐

DATE

_____

81

STORY ☐ INVENTION ☐ INNOVATION ☐

DATE

_____

82

STORY ☐   INVENTION ☐   INNOVATION ☐

DATE

_____

83

STORY ☐   INVENTION ☐   INNOVATION ☐

DATE

_____

84

STORY ☐ INVENTION ☐ INNOVATION ☐

DATE

_____

85

STORY □   INVENTION □   INNOVATION □

DATE

_____

STORY ☐ INVENTION ☐ INNOVATION ☐

DATE

_____

87

STORY ☐   INVENTION ☐   INNOVATION ☐

DATE

_____

88

STORY ☐ INVENTION ☐ INNOVATION ☐

DATE

_____

STORY □ INVENTION □ INNOVATION □

DATE

_____

STORY ☐ INVENTION ☐ INNOVATION ☐

DATE

91

STORY ☐   INVENTION ☐   INNOVATION ☐

DATE

_____

STORY ☐   INVENTION ☐   INNOVATION ☐

DATE

_____

93

STORY INVENTION INNOVATION

DATE

_____

94

STORY ☐ INVENTION ☐ INNOVATION ☐

DATE

_____

STORY   INVENTION   INNOVATION
☐   ☐   ☐

DATE

_____

96

STORY ☐   INVENTION ☐   INNOVATION ☐

DATE

_____

STORY ☐ INVENTION ☐ INNOVATION ☐

DATE

_____

98

STORY □ INVENTION □ INNOVATION □

DATE

_____

STORY ☐   INVENTION ☐   INNOVATION ☐

DATE

_____

AN ALL SORTS PAGE.

AN ALL SORTS PAGE.

13208360R00060

Printed in Great Britain
by Amazon